The Conclusion of the WHOLE MATTER

WORSHIP

ZEALOUS PRAISE

PSALMS   POETRY   PROSE

Lillie M. White

To order additional copies of this book, contact:
Xlibris
1-888-795-4274
www.Xlibris.com
Orders@Xlibris.com

All Scripture quotations are from the King James Version of the Bible

ISBN: Softcover   978-1-4628-9616-5
         EBook   978-1-7960-6906-8

Print information available on the last page

Rev. date: 10/29/2019

The effectual fervent prayer of a righteous [woman] availeth much (James 5:16)

...praise is comely......(PS 33:1)

CONTENTS

PROSE

IN MEMORY OF

A HEDGE

Thou hast made an hedge about [her],
and about [her] house, and about all that
[she] hath on every side. Thou hast blessed
the work of [her] hands, and [her] substance
is increased in the land.
Job 1:10 The Holy Bible, King James Version

WELCOME

"Welcome into my Father's House. In
every color you will see him. In every
corner He is there. For He is living not dead!"

There is one body, and one Spirit, even as
ye are called in one hope of your calling;
One Lord, one faith, one baptism,

One God and Father of all
Who is above all, and through all,
and in you all.
Eph 4:4, 5, 6 Holy Bible, King James Version

WELCOME

Welcome into my Father's House
In every corner you will see Him
In every color He is there

Welcome into my Father's House for this is where
He dwells. They say that He has left us
Not so say I
A loving parent remains even when confusion abides

Welcome I say welcome
Into a house of love
Here dwells my Heavenly Father
On earth from heaven above.

Welcome!

"Let HIM Kiss Me"
HALLELUJAH
when thanks turns into tremendous love (Song 1:2)

Oh **JEHO VAH,** how sweet is the love i have for YOU its more than anything

I feel YOU in the morning breeze and falling of the autumn leaves

In the winter's frozen frost and frigid winds that turn my breath to ice......................when i talk

And when YOU shine YOUR light i lift my hands with pure delight!!!

Oh **JEHO VAH**

no other voice I need to say

I

love

YAH

Yes, I love YOU

THE HOLY KISS

This is a kiss of life and blessings. This brings pleasures
unimaginable. This kiss says because you have loved me I will
love you. This kiss illuminates and heals everything that is
broken is made whole. The Holy kiss of the anointed of God is
immeasurable in its restoring and life giving properties for it is
the kiss of Love…

GOD IS LOVE

THE KISS OF GREETINGS

This is a welcoming kiss. A kiss that says *"enter in, enjoy yourself,*

Make yourself at *home. We want you in our presence."*

There is nothing we have that will be withheld from you.

You are our FRIEND *(brethren)*

THE SATANIC KISS

You know this kiss the one that Judas gave Christ at the Last Supper.

A Kiss full of hidden agendas, this kiss lives today, manifested on TV, movies, computers screens and all print media

Luring us further into *abominable physical abnormal* uses of our *holy temples.......so* much so......that THE

FATHER OF LIGHT cannot abide there

but the father of darkness can.

BLESSED

Blessed is the child with the spirit
of life in his eyes.

Blessed is the woman with the womb
that carries life.

Blessed is the man with the seed
of life.

Blessed is the day for the sun that
shines on everyone

and Blessed am I, for today, I live.

KNOWLEDGE

Give me knowledge so I
might not despair this
human condition I must bear.

If only I could comprehend
The reasons why even the purist
of souls must undergo sorrows
and burdens they do not owe.

Give me knowledge so I might
end the confusion the world is in.

At least, Oh Lord, if this you
cannot do, give me simple
understanding to last until
my day is thru.

THANK YOU FATHER

I am in continued awe of Thee
I look upon this cold, misty, gray rainy day
And still see the splendor of You

May I extol you, my Lord, my King
In Your awesomeness

I feel You in the storm and tempest wind
Rain as it did in the beginning when water came up
as a midst to water the earth

Now Lord, send the rain down to bless us. All
creation drink of Your mercy

The fowl of the air praise with early morning songs
blessing you with searched out wings, soaring,
feeling The Spirit In The Air

All creatures chrip with delight at the coming
of Your healing light
We the wordly congregation lift up our hands
humbly bow and say

Thank You Father
Thank You Abba
Thank You O Ancient Of Days

They Who Judge

I live in a world of self proclaimed
deities and man made omnipotence.

They scorn me with their eyes,
they blaspheme, they utter lies.

But I do not shrink and wither before their sight.

For it is the Creator who has deemed that I should be.

So, I laugh, I dance, I sing.

And I invite, all to see, the living

God, who lives in me!

A WIFE'S PRAYER

In this hour of testing, Oh **LORD**
give me the strength to stand

That I might endure all the fiery darts
let not my heart waver

Give me the love needed to strengthen the heart of my husband
That he know the love of his Creator in me
God so loved the world that HE gave...............

Let me therefore so love and give to this man
I humbly pray

FATHER lift us up in the palm of YOUR right hand

All glory to your NAME

                  Selah!!!

WHITE LIGHT
OF THE HOLY SPIRIT

White Light of the Holy Spirit
Resonating, illuminating from deep within
turning the hate, the sin into a love that heals all men

The Lord can put a stop to this with
the sound of HIS voice

      I speak to the North, West, East and South
      Life Come Out!!!
      out of the death, the pain
      Let Purity live again!!!

White Light of the Holy Spirit
Sanitize us, wash us clean
let your healing powers flow

Wipe away sin, pain, disease
bring us back to THEE!!!

White Light of the Holy Spirit
Resonating, Illuminating from deep within
turning the hate
      the sin
         into a love
            That Heals All men

Solitary/Oneness

Being alone with one's self is the ultimate test.

Solitary confinement, where soldiers and generals
break kings.

What an adversary to defeat, the one who lives
inside, the one who knows all the reasons why you cry.

But when he is defeated and his nagging voice is Stilled

The accuser of the brethren who set out to kill your
soul has fallen into his own accusatory net and lost
his very own. *(PS 7:15)*

For as it is written now so it is
Those who love the Lord, shall forever live.

AIDS

The plague that lurks in the darkness
ravaging the body and mind from an
Intimacy GOD declared divine

Satan hand on the most sacred part of man
his scheming plot, his envious plans for the demise of
that creature called man

But GOD can heal that creature
HE can heal the land
GOD can stop satan's sinister plans

The body is formed in the image of love
Every rot flesh purged with hyppso from above
Washed and made whole

He cleanses the body
He cleanses the mind
He cleanses the soul

This the CREATOR can do

For me

And

For you!!!

FAMILY VALUES

What is a civilization but a group of people that hold a set
of standards which they proudly announce "we are civilized".

But a civilization, in its most basic form is nothing more
than a family.

Nothing flourishes more, nothing grows strong,

But that which is showered with love, care and acceptance.

Family values is the making of a civilization, the making of
a strong man, a strong woman, a strong child.

God blesses the family that is rooted in love.

HOPE

Caught up in a sea of benevolence
Founded on your many dreams of tomorrow
Hope comes.

It tarries not.

Like the dawn of a new day,
like a bird flying motionlessly
against a blue and white clouded day
hope comes.

It shatters the walls of discontentment,
shatters the walls of hopelessness,
shatters the barricades of your mind,
hope comes.

Hope comes at the end when you thought
There was no more.
Hope lives and keeps you alive.
Hope speaks when no one answers.

Hope is Almighty!

Hope is God!

POETRY

MAN/WOMAN

He saw her gazing at him
there was such adoration in
her eyes as if she were looking
at a King.

He thought if she see this it
must be. His head lifted, shoulders
pulled back and he became King.

She saw him gazing at her
there was such adoration in
his eyes as if he were looking
at a priceless jewel.

She thought if he see this it
must be. Her head lifted and
she walked elegantly by and became
that priceless jewel.

It is true the man makes the woman
and the woman makes the man

PURPLE

(Kata Markon)

I want to rest in the color of passion and purpose
to know the excellence of YOU
Sovereign and Whole
Restoration of mind body and soul
It is Spring!!!

AUTUMN

It's in the beauty of the trees
the every changing colors of the leaves
how nature is so like me

The emotions fire and ice blended together to make
me what I am

God! how I love the changing hues
a momentary vision of what I am
for tomorrow will be something new

Surrounded by glory, I am the earth, the sun, the sea

The universe is wrapped up in a small little
package called **me!!!**

VIRTUE

In a time of great temptation, a pandora's
Box beckons me. It teasingly temps me
with promises of all physical gratification,
all curiosity satisfied, all material needs met.

I open this box, of human treasures and
a metamorphosis occurs. I become all
knowing, mysteries and secrets are no more.
I look into the mirror and see innocence
gone. It has been replaced with a
stately grace, an educated calm.

Do you recognize it?

Can you see?
Virtue become me!

HEIGHTS

I looked up one day and
saw a butterfly. I watched
it as it crossed the clear
blue sky. It landed on a
tree branch. Its wings spread
open wide displaying all its colors.

I could not reach it for it
was way too high, but I was
content to watch. Oh, how the
colors lifted me. I felt it
was I. I spread my arms as
it began to fly.

There were so many colors that
I felt. The serenity of blue, the
fiery heat of red, mystery of
black, innocents of pink and
finally the royalty of silvery gold.

Oh, what delight to reach
for and obtain a mental height.

Woman

A woman now, I was not then childish dreams and
Childish thoughts, youthful awakenings of things that were not.

The years have come and gone. Time has passed me by.
I regret not the things I did not achieve but am hopeful the future I
will see.

A woman now, I was not then a selfish child lived

within but in the course of time, I came to see the world
was not mine but to be shared with all mandkind. I stand
proud and free, with much to give, a loving heart to
strengthen anyone who is opened enough to feel.

I am woman.

My love is real

MOTHER

I gave birth to sons!

One, black as midnight, loved by the sun.
One, white as snow, glorious to behold.
One, smooth and round, he was brown.
The other red, from all the blood I shed.

I raised my sons in love. They all drank the milk of
nourishment and grew strong.

Sibling rivalry came along. They taunted each other
unmercifully. I would scorn "love your brother, he to I have born!"

Came the day my sons went their separate ways.
I go east and I go west. "So far from your brother, do you think
that is best?" The others said "I go north and I go south".

I watched my sons ride off in all different directions.
Tears swelled in my eyes.

I knelt down to pray.

"Please Lord, bring my sons back together, one day!"

AIN'T I TO A WOMAN

Ain't I to a woman

Don't I need protection too

Ain't my babies allowed to love me

Don't my babies need their mamas like you

Africa mama's calling you

Abandoned   and   Forgotten

Loss   and   Alone

Used   and   Abused

Terrorized   and   Ouster zed

Ain't got no home!

Global community I say to you

Ain't I
Ain't I
Ain't I
A woman too!!!

IF WORDS COULD KILL

If words could kill we've
died a million times. The unconsious
blood we've shed.
I've shed yours and you've shed mine.

We talk of love and know not the
meaning of the word.

My subconsious heart beat begins
to fade from the harsh cruel words
you say.

.. But I place no blame on you
For I am guilty too.

Like a witch. I saw you as my
prey. I stripped your manhood
away and sent your self-esteem
to its grave.

Do you think one day, we
will be able to say, we gave
love and not that we took love
away.

DIVORCE

It was the delusion that I embraced.

My greatest enjoyment was
my deception.

And now, years have
unfolded all untrues, and
left me in horror, of the reality
that I am alone!

Love was never mine, but
lust the culprit in disguise.

Bitter its fruit and fatal its bite,
death comes easily now like a
blanket of night.

I sit and mourn love 's death.

How long, I have waited for this final
release! Forever peace, what a
consolation for a heart that cannot mend.

MANCHILD
SONS OF MY WOMB

My hands wrapped around my swollen belly and screams of pain
pain only a woman knows

Weak and exhausted, my voice reduced to just a moan
I hear the crying of a child, a man child
what joy, joy only a mother knows

Now stands before me a man
where once stood a child and
in the twilight hours I talk to GOD above

Bless this man, this child with love
I have done all that I can do
the umbilical cord is broken

Life is his
        good
                or
                        bad
It is all left unspoken

ENTITY

In the body of a woman I came
the year 1800 my name Sarah Bartmann.
They exhibited me on showroom floors.
Strange hands stroked my buttocks and fondled my breast
I cried out "Where is my man?"
In this body I could not stay
I slipped into a forever rest.

Again I came
I made it to the age of 33
My name Phyllis Wheatley.

Again in a woman strong and stout
In the Congress Halls I shouted out
"Ain't I to a woman?" Sojourn Truth
My words fell on deaf ears.

Millennium is here
I Lillie White come to say
I am a woman to be protected
and respected, my love is not for public view
I come to stand not behind
but on side of you.

PRIMAL SCREAM

They marched in Tennemen Square
and bullets polluted the air. When it
was over, there lay the bodies. And
from across the seas I heard their
primal scream

It was the same cry of Bishop Tu Tu
when he said "end apartheid now!"
I heard his primal scream.

It is the same cry of the homeless mother
moving her children from one shelter to
another, lost in economic poverty
I hear her primal scream.

It is the same cry as the junky strung out
on dope in search of another high
lost in a chemical existence
I hear his primal scream

And time goes on
days turn into years
Millennium is here and in the distance
I hear a muffled sound
growing louder and louder
it is the primal scream

       FREEDOM!!!

PROSE

FIVE DAYS OF GRACE

**EVENTS LEADING UP TO THE ELECTION OF
THE FIRST AFRICAN AMERICAN PRESIDENT**

FRIDAY
October 31, 2008

In five days we select a new President and Leader of the free world. I am in intercession for a Barack Obama victory. It will conclude three months of fasting. I am confident that my prayers have been answered. Now just walking out the preliminaries, five days of grace. What do I expect? What most Americans are looking for, end of war and loss of young life. Hope for improvements in our economy and stop the siphoning of wealth from the American people.

SATURDAY
November 01, 2008

Much excitement is in the air! Wonderful hope is in the hearts of the people. Hilary Clinton came to town and our future President will be here Sunday evening. America is a woman in Travail, what will She bring forth?

SUNDAY
November 02, 2008

Today was a day of praise, the service was full of jubilee. We danced and praised for the manifested blessing. After service we all went to different locations around the city. My team went to Batavia. The Spirit of the Lord fell as we prayed for that area. The sun shone so bright, we all commented on the light.

MONDAY
November 03. 2008

I got up and went to work at the school for Creative and Preforming Arts. It went well, I subbed for Mr. Hand. After work I went to the NAACP meeting with Mr. Smitherman, the local president. We planned for election day. After the meeting his assistant took me home.

TUESDAY
November 04, 2008

I woke, dressed and hurried to my polling place. It was an unusually warm day, the temp would get up to 75 degrees. I was excited about the outcome of the day, Barack Obama will be our next President.

I arrived at MT Airy School. I met two friends also working the polls. A man from New York worked on side of us. Around noon, the guard came out of the building, she ordered us to move our Barack Obama signs. We did.

By evening a moderate flow of people kept coming. I noticed a voter very upset. I asked why and he said this was his third time trying to vote. So I said come on lets find out what's wrong. We went back in and the poll worker said they had made a mistake. He voted.

7:30 pm the polls closed and I went with a NAACP member to a local restaurant. We watched the outcome with Mr Smitherman and the NAACP team. We all cheered Barack Obama was leading and so was our issues/red light cameras and portional representation. Calls started coming in, the jubilation mounted. Mr Smitherman announced we would be moving to Integrity Hall.

A member of the NAACP offered to take me home (*at that time I had no car*). I accepted.

11:30 pm the announcement came over the radio *"BARACK OBAMA IS THE PRESIDENT OF THE UNITED STATES OF AMERICA!"*
I called all my friends and shouted (*in my voice echoed the voices of the ancestors*) ALLELUIA!!!

The fast ended, in the words of my bishop **"God did that thing!!!"**

EGYPT IS FREE!
CELEBRATE

The military was standing by as Egyptians filled the streets.
FREEDOM WAS THEIR PASSION CRY!
No bullets flew for the soldiers shared their hunger too

As they bowed and prayed to THE MOST HIGH
their prayers echoed all over the world and throughout all time

"FREEDOM WE MUST HAVE OR WE DIE!"
"FREEDOM IS OUR PASSION CRY!"

Came those who did oppose
tried to put out the flames, stomp the souls, kill the desire
Yes, blood did flow

The wounded held up their battle scars to show they have tasted
freedom's promise and smelled its sweet winds of change
Their response a defiant cry "We won't go!
We are prepared to die for freedom is our right!

They bowed again and prayed
18 days went by and like JERICHO
Mubarack had to go! The walls came tumbling down
He couldn't stay for GOD HIMSELF said "ENOUGH!"

And

FREEDOM CAME THAT DAY!!!

(2-11-11)

IN BETWEEN PLACE

When your in that place, the in between place, the here and there, the seen and unseen. In that place you are closest to God and His adversary. In that place, God shows you the traps that snare His people. He takes you to the high places, allows you to stare into the face of the ungodly. But He doesn't leave you in the abyss. Once you have overcome the shock of the darkness, He enables you to speak life and call out every evil thing. You become a purifier, a conduit for His mercy, allowing light to dispel the dark.

IN MEMORY OF

A TRIBUTE

Frederick Lamar White
Sunrise Dec 18, 1971 - Sunset Jan 10, 2010

FOR MY LOVE ONES GONE

THEY LIVE ON……….. IN MY HEART

THREE

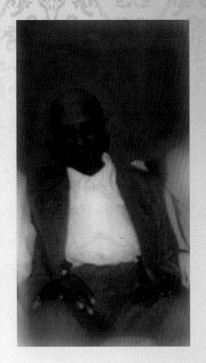

FACES

OF
WISDOM

OLD GRAY EYES

James Harrison Murphy

He speaks of times gone by
of Marcus Garvey and going back to Africa
Of a father who didn't want him
Of a mother who gave him away because he
was too dark. Now well into his hundreds, he
sits in his rocker and his mind drifts
"It's Lillie Pop, your great granddaughter
named after your wife great grandma."

"Lillie?"

"Yes Pop."

"Give her power, give her overcoming power
that Your name shall have the praise!"

These were words I heard often as a child
for he was a healer in his day
He caresses me with his old gray eyes.

I wonder.....

Where is he now?
Carrying the hard, making dandelion wine
singing in his triumphant voice
as he slips somewhere between the earthly and heavenly realm
How proud I am, to have come from the loins of such
a great man.

Rest Pop!
Rest now!
For you are,

HEAVEN BOUND!!!

MUD

Rich earth, dark, black, fertile

Strength to nourish crops, fields, towns, cities

Civilizations

Trees of cedar send their roots deep into her.

Trees that bend but do not break weathering the

STORMS

Oh! What fertile ground

MUD!!!

AUNT RACHEL
"BOOTS"

To all my family and friends to you
I say.... I came to my end

It was that old body
you see.... that just kept stopping the party
Now I'm dancing and laughing
haven a good old time

I got my crown!!!

Don't be crying, live your life and do the best you can
I'm going back to the heavenly feast
see ya when ya get here

Meanwhile I'll be sending my love
when you see a bird, a flower, the sun and trees
just give a little wink and think of me

Boots is free!!!

THE ROSE OF SHARON

The Rose of Sharon smiles at me everyday. Soft was
her voice, a melody of truth.

She walked in the garden, so was her grace that
animals sought comfort in her space.

She walked with his presence by her side. Lived out
her years in glory until He spoke "Come rest in me. "

My Rose of Sharon looked up to me and said, "You
. too will come and be by His side. " Silently, she said
"goodbye. "

But the trumpets blew and angels sang, the heavens
opened up and victory rang.

She sits at the side of the King!

My Rose of Sharon sings!!!

MISS CARROLL

A song of praise emitted the day Miss Carroll went away.

Out came the sun and shined so clean, fresh and bright.

Only Miss Carroll could have ordered such divine
light, a benediction sent to bless all the ones she loved.

She was that way.

Tears fell from my eyes for I knew no longer would I
see Jesus in her eyes.

But because I knew her well, I heard
her Spirit say"
live your life child, I'd want it
that way."

The sun radiated, a celestial
light, The day, Miss
Carroll went away.

Selah!

A PATRIOTIC FAMILY
SERVING SINCE WORLD WAR 11

MILITARY SALUTE

TO

MARYELLEN ROBINSON

(GREAT AUNT MAE)

CHARLES EUGENE WHITE JR.

JAMES ANTHONY WHITE

SPECIAL PRAISE

1st Black Female Army
Company 6,3rd Reg. W.A.C Oct. 9, 1944
Aunt Mae in circle

Charles Eugene White Jr.

James Anthony White

SPECIAL PRAISE

VETERANS

STANDING STRONG TO PROTECT

GIVING THEIR VERY LIVES

AND YET.......

I stand with uplifted hands

To say Thank You, for being true

I love you Army, Navy, Marines

For doing the best you can

Giving more than any ordinary man or woman

Laying down your lives for us the sheep

Lord please help them to stand

Protect them as they fight

FOR OUR RIGHTS

AND

WAY OF LIFE